ALSO BY MARY JO SALTER

POEMS

Zoom Rooms (2022)

The Surveyors (2017)

Nothing by Design (2013)

A Phone Call to the Future: New and Selected Poems (2008)

Open Shutters (2003)

A Kiss in Space (1999)

Sunday Skaters (1994)

Unfinished Painting (1989)

Henry Purcell in Japan (1985)

FOR CHILDREN

The Moon Comes Home (1989)

CAMEO APPEARANCE

CAMEO APPEARANCE

POEMS

Mary Jo Salter

ALFRED A. KNOPF NEW YORK 2026

A BORZOI BOOK
FIRST HARDCOVER EDITION
PUBLISHED BY ALFRED A. KNOPF 2026

Published by Alfred A. Knopf,
a division of Penguin Random House LLC,
1745 Broadway, New York, NY 10019.

Knopf, Borzoi Books, and the colophon are registered
trademarks of Penguin Random House LLC.

Library of Congress Cataloging-in-Publication Data
Names: Salter, Mary Jo, author
Title: Cameo appearance : poems / Mary Jo Salter.
Other titles: Cameo appearance (Compilation)
Description: First hardcover edition. | New York : Alfred A. Knopf, 2026.
Identifiers: LCCN 2025045707 (print) | LCCN 2025045708 (ebook) |
ISBN 9780593804766 hardcover | ISBN 9780593804773 ebook
Subjects: LCGFT: Poetry
Classification: LCC PS3569.A46224 C36 2026 (print) | LCC PS3569.A46224 (ebook)
LC record available at https://lccn.loc.gov/2025045707
LC ebook record available at https://lccn.loc.gov/2025045708

penguinrandomhouse.com | aaknopf.com

Printed in the United States of America
1st Printing

The authorized representative in the EU for product safety and compliance is
Penguin Random House Ireland, Morrison Chambers,
32 Nassau Street, Dublin D02 YH68, Ireland,
https://eu-contact.penguin.ie.

For Edward Garner Cowart
and Elinora Gladys Leithauser

Contents

7

1

HOME OFFICE

Four-sixteen in the morning.
Mutual facial

recognition established
with my cell phone.

I slip out of the covers, tiptoe
down to the desk

tucked under the staircase,
to the laptop where I type

a rhyme that clicks in the moonlight:
mute commute.

Exactly! For a moment
I've understood what I meant.

Then I've lost it. Still half-dreaming.
Everything means something

declares now the astonishing
swiveling creature spotted

up there in a tree: the barred
owl in aviator glasses

riveted, it appears, to the mouse
in my restless hand.

FULL MOON

The first time, late in the afternoon,
we saw the full moon,
it was lifting its chin
just above the horizon.

Against the pearl-gray silk of sky
it was pale and thin
as a mother-of-pearl button.

We parked and went into the supermarket.
Thought of the moon and then forgot.
With a neutral sort of cheer, we bought
some necessary stuff, plus a treat
or two to compensate for—what?
I felt it but couldn't say.

The second time we saw the full moon,
an hour or so on,
it had already risen
halfway up a blue-black sky;
its glow had begun to intensify;
it had rounded the third dimension.

It was so lovely I had to cry
"Look at the moon!" as if you or I
might never see one again.

Then you drove and we talked about politics.
With people, sublimity never sticks.
The woods on either side of the road
got darker and thicker
while the moon, fragmented, flickering

among the trees, remained content
not to be seen, omniscient,
nodding overhead.

CAMEO APPEARANCE

White image on blue Wedgwood
of a woman in upswept
coiffure and full-length gown,

corseted silhouette
with a coy bulge of bustle,
her shape went out of style

well before my flapper
grandmother was given
this ring that now is mine.

Has been mine for fifty years—
no time, that is; the gap
is the same between her prime

and this lady's, one in which
it apparently was normal,
fist under chin, to rest

an elbow on an amphora
nearly her height, and wait.
For what? Perhaps the thought

that the past is all one era,
may as well be ancient Greece
with its own painted figures

of gods and warriors
chasing each other round
and round some empty jars.

For years, fearing this band
of silver might slip off
somewhere, I let it sleep

in a box—until I woke
one morning to discover
my own ring-finger knuckle

had grown the size of hers
and I had come full circle,
had married my grandmother.

Where did they all go,
my go-go boots, bell-bottoms,
shoulder pads, opinions,

boyfriends, favorite songs,
and other newly minted
traits no longer current

or even of account
to what I call my self?
They might be anyone's,

may or may not surface
as evidence, an essence
of a generation almost

nobody but those
born into it can compass
even for a minute:

a ring, some other thing
a descendant can be proud of
because it isn't lost.

AQUEDUCT

All the other professors emeriti
have shuffled in, neat in jacket and tie
except for the few ladies (flats and hose),
and everyone's in hearing aids—both those
with hair to hide the wires and those without,
and (a subcategory) those who shout
their greetings now while sporting a severe
kind of stopper, jammed into the ear
as if to bar the spillage of what remains
(old wine in old bottles) of their brains.
These are his people. And as in a bad dream
all of them are assembled to hear *him*.

Why worry? Hell, he has the material cold—
one of the perks, he thinks, of getting old.
True, it's been harder lately to acquire
new knowledge, but he took the Roman Empire
as his dissertation's massive territory
when a young man, then inched beyond that story
until he'd conquered all. Two score and ten
years later and, by God, the thing is written.
People at the university press,
young editors with Ph.D.s, said yes,
his book—historiography, if you will,
an account of all accounts—shows scope and skill

not seen in ages. So again: why worry?
This crowd, his crowd, is hardly in a hurry
and actually looking forward to his talk.
What was he thinking, though, that he could walk
up here in his ancient sweatshirt (as he might

drift into the kitchen late at night,
uncertain how he got there) with a few
pages of notes? In fact, he has no clue
who introduced him, or when he began to speak,
but he can tell from their faces it's a weak
case he's been presenting, sweating, flustered,
paragraphs of filler filibustered

while he searches for one word. What delivers
water on an arched thing down from rivers
to cross a valley? . . . At home in his study
he has the time, thesaurus, and the steady
belief in himself to find such . . . Aqueduct!
Aqueduct! Oh, he's well and truly fucked,
he can't go on pretending to be pensive
when word retrieval fails, or sound defensive
in his final lecture—apparently today
A modest drop of charm, then, in Q & A:
"Excellent question, thank you, Chuck. I knew
you'd think of that, but it's beyond my purview."

Blandly they nod, blankly they smile and clap
a smattering of applause before they tap
away on their canes. Some in the club were worse,
he tells himself; their own retirement lectures
drowned in minutiae, diverted from arguments,
wallowed in moot points . . . yet what sense
in dwelling on them? Rather dream this dream
of driving their rented Peugeot in from Nîmes
on their honeymoon—before the debris and silt
of years clogged up what he, like Rome, had built—
to see the magnificent Pont du Gard, the blue
sky behind tiers of arches pouring through
like fluent water.

PAX ROMANA

I'm about to take a photograph
of a little girl playing alone in the sand
that surrounds the Arc de Triomphe d'Orange,
where Tiberius Caesar glorified
the victories of Germanicus.

I've studied on its outer sides
the bas-reliefs of clashing shields,
strangely abstract and disembodied
given how desperately soldiers
scrambled in the howling chaos

to seize upon split-second chances
to pierce or find yourself pierced: a horror
more immediate on the frieze
of balletic, profiled butchery
that runs across the pediment.

From where I stand, just far enough
away not to worry her mother, who strolls
the baby in loops around and through
the ancient arches, all the while
keeping the four-year-old in view,

her tiny, engrossing toy, bright yellow
and cherry red, is a candy wrapper
repurposed as a monument.
She's speaking French to it, and softly.
She is inventing origami,

folding her waxy square of paper
to make a sharper peak for the roof.
As I lift my phone to take the shot,
her finger drags through the sand to enclose
her work in a perfect circle.

AN ALLEY IN AVIGNON

November tourist, muscling my way through
the mistral, guidebook in hand, I turned in to
a wind-tunnel alley, looking for 22
rue du Roi René, which as I knew

no longer marked the cloister of St. Clare.
Fitting, I thought, they'd built a theater
in its place, pleasing us arty types who'd care
Petrarch recorded he first saw Laura there.

And recorded and recorded. So many rhymes
and plays on her name, lauded so many times
as the sun and sum of all being, here she seems
solid as the church bell that now chimes

thrillingly on cue, only a block
or two away. I'm standing before the plaque
on the theater's stone façade; it says that back
in 1327, when he took

one look at her that Good Friday, he was gone.
What does it really mean to love someone?
Am I serious, asking this? I'm sixty-nine,
the age he died, I understand convention,

crave it in fact. This one's courtly love,
the beautiful bow to beauty set above
all others, the de rigueur frustration of
desire, his pining even for her glove

which of course she denies, and despite the birth
of eleven children and a ghastly death
(at thirty-eight, of the plague), her perfect youth
surviving, the least mortal thing on earth.

She'd married, or some scholars say she had,
an ancestor of the Marquis de Sade,
or maybe hadn't. Old archives are so bad
when it comes to women, sometimes you're just glad

there's a tale to tell, however apocryphal.
And Petrarch's children's mother—whom no legal
tie ever bound, whose name's illegible
to time, of whom no fact is known at all?—

I see her bring him candles he will light
one on another, staying up late to write
what she couldn't read but heard about, and might
well star the peerless Laura, who tonight
again he'll fall for, here, and at first sight.

2

CHRIST TAKING LEAVE OF HIS MOTHER

Gerard David

The two tiny paintings
of the portable diptych

long ago took leave of each other—
so I'm staring at only

a single perfection,
Christ Taking Leave of His Mother,

set on a pedestal in the heart
of a room in the Met

devoted to devotional
objects made for those bigwigs who

had had the means to buy them,
and to travel,

as I have done:
taking the train deliberately

up the coast to Penn Station
and its hall named for Moynihan,

bow-tied patron saint
of improvement;

boarding the subway,
storing my bag at the hotel

(not yet time for check-in),
getting on and off

one more subway line,
crossing avenues in long strides

finally to arrive at the grand
pyramidal staircase

to the pillared temple,
and evading the crowds

snaking up those steps,
taking the lesser-known entrance

on the ground floor,
flashing my out-of-towner's

membership card
and asking a guard

yet again (I've never had
a sense of direction)

where in this vast emporium
I can find the room

that moved me so last time.

•

And here I am.

I'm bending my head
to peer into the cube of glass

in which four heads the size
of nickels bend

to fit within their gilded arch.
Christ raises one hand

in the usual blessing,
but also like a bored young man

waving away his mother's worry—
Catch you later,

I'm off to Jerusalem—
and even she,

the pale fingertips
of her two hands touching

in an act of prayer
the little panel's purchaser

would have emulated,
wears the weary look

beneath her hood
of centuries of acceptance.

It's a departure, I've read,
among the many

variations on this theme
turned out by David

and his workshop and other
“mass reproductions” of their time,

to include in the son-
and-mother scene

Martha and Mary Magdalene;
but here they are,

jammed into their golden room
like us museumgoers, who

are used to partial masterpieces
because other people

are in the way:
what Martha’s two eyes strain to see

(we have to imagine
her nose and chin

behind the head of the Virgin)
is blocked by the figure

of Mary Magdalene,
who says goodbye

with a diaphanous handkerchief
dabbing at one eye.

Ah, this is it.
This is why I've come.

This is the very essence of grief,
her one tear even heavier

for not being seen,
nor the many more

she has in her;
the misery in her looking not

directly at him one last time
but down, so as

not to face
his indifference to her beauty;

her effort to contain
herself when what she loves

the most now must
for some greater good

that others apparently understand
(no, she refuses to pretend

she has understood)
be taken away forever.

It occurs to me
I've stayed marveling

at this gemlike thing
a long, long time,

almost giddy I've lived
to pay my dues to sorrow

yet another day.
I could, if I chose,

come back tomorrow—
although I fathomed

in her expression just how rare
the creatures are

who have the gift to remain
in a heightened state

indefinitely;
the rest go home on the train.

3

NOT ON SPEAKING TERMS

Walking through weeks and weeks
with a rock in the heart—
no, not the left side or the right
but the choked-up center,
the rock in the esophagus,
a rock I didn't ask to eat
and cannot swallow
or spit out—

that's what your law forbidding talk
feels like to me.
That's what never hearing what
you're not saying but
are thinking, in what I only guess
is a helpless whirligig of fury,
feels like to me:
an emptiness

like the absences in outer space,
but black-hole heavy.
Nothing is heavier
than this, the rock
that blocks me says;
don't even try
crying *it isn't fair, it isn't fair*
into the unforgiving air.

REFLECTIONS

The man himself!—or in any case an image
on my laptop of his real-time form, five hours
later in England but also here and now,
peering at us from his computer screen
and lowering his head to an unseen
novel on his desk, to read aloud

to a virtual audience of writers
(many of whom had tried this very day
to conjure at our screens a thing that's true
about living, in words true as we could find)
a few scenes from *Atonement*. I had read it
twice before, had seen the movie; now,

in a livestream of a graying, mild guy reading
his novel with commentary, I heard him say
that the headstrong, teenaged writer Briony—
who, in the book, would spend her life to come
atoning for one wrongful act by writing
this book itself, one with a happy ending

that unhappily was all made up—was not
always meant by him to be the author.
It came to him midway, part of the process.
Ghostwriter, that's what he'd become, and even
willed for himself: to appear to disappear.
Or that's what I was thinking at the moment

fifty minutes in when finally
I saw what had been mirrored all along
in the window of night sky behind his head:

our Zoom-heads, one moon centered in each mullion.
His monitor's reflection in that window,
blocked partly by the shadow of the body

who sat before it, proved I was in England
gazing at me here, however blurry.
Infinite fictions! Yet time for only one
last question. *Mr. McEwan,* someone asks,
what do you think you've learned of what it means
to be sorry; to atone? A thoughtful answer

emerges, touching on Henry James, James Joyce,
the examined life. "You can't call back the deeds,"
the author says. And pious self-forgiveness,
he tends to think, is too easy a way out.
He pauses, offers a smile that reads as rueful.
"All you can do is contemplate. Reflect."

VACCINE

I remember when they jabbed her
hard, through her little thigh:
it made me cry.

Now it's her turn to bear
her baby's turn. To take it in
that she can't win,

she has to do what hurts, and
not explain;
and never have the words

though she has plenty;
though all new parents say
new words all day.

RECOVERY

When I hear
recuperate,
I taste a *cup*
of tea in it
and more in the pot,

I think *recap*—
as if you will
reclaim the person
you were when well;
and also *copper,*

Cu and a cue
to picture a thin
rust-colored bracelet
meant to conquer
the bones' deep pain.

Not so *recover.*
Sure, its Latin
roots are the same,
but the word, I find,
gets at some punishing

thing in the mind
that's bound to happen
at three in the morning
time and again—
what makes you cower

under the covers
although the saner
part of you knows
there's no intruder
(yet) in the house.

TWO REFUSALS

I.

My first began with green
zigzags like the line
up-downing on the Dow.
I couldn't see, so how
could I doomscroll my condition?
I gave in, closed my eyes;
in time the nightmare vision
of neon graphs was gone.

Then I met with Dr. Chan
(in the cutest turquoise shoes
with satin bows at the toes:
oh, grant me yet more years
of joy in the world's colors!),
who said a luckily pain-
free "ocular migraine"
was the likely diagnosis.

Advice? A long, unwitting
joke, her list of common
triggers to avoid:
under- or overeating,
too much, too little sleep,
hormonal changes (sorry,
that menopausal ship
sailed long ago for me);

also, she continued,
changes in medication,
changes in the weather
(can I stop the rain?),
and stress. Cut it altogether
along with its cure, red wine.
I smiled at her shoes and nodded.
Sure, is what I said.

2.

Sleep apnea split my nights
into catnaps. An apparatus
with a pleated breathing tube
like the coil that sucks exhausted
hot air from the dryer
was meant to prevent a stroke
or heart attack, but wrapped
itself around my neck.
For weeks I'd lie on my back,
entangled, nearly strangled,
thinking of all the torture
methods of the past.
Who wouldn't prefer the rack?

Enough. I drove to the clinic
and returned the vile device.
May it rest in peace
and may the man I defied,
a glum pulmonologist
who didn't fool me, but tried
his hardest to pretend
he wouldn't judge my choice,
blot me from consciousness.
I aim to do that myself.
Whenever now I choke
myself awake, I vow
not to succumb to panic

and slip out of bed, believing
that love is also leaving
a husband to his slumber.
I mosey to the kitchen
to make some tea or cocoa;
if there's a donut, I down it.
Then I stretch out on the sofa,
where I turn on a whodunit.
I've drifted off to them all—
soon after the first scene
of somebody's bloody end
which happens not to be mine.
And waking up is fine.

OUTSIDE READING

Curious always
as the buck that came munching
the thorniest vines,

then planted himself
and his branches of antlers
smack in the middle

of our little lawn,
you turn one more page in your
difficult book while

a finger of breeze
tries to get your attention,
lifts hairs on your arms.

What's so consuming?
I do want to know, and feel
happy not asking.

Or so I'm musing
at the dining room window
as you're looking up

to follow the drift
of a leaf come to bookmark
the place in your lap.

DEAD FAMILY MEMBERS

Billy Collins, in an interview
I read today (duly "edited
for brevity and clarity")
said, "I believe that family members
can burden a poem, especially
if they happen to be dead."
He went on, "So if I come across
'Daddy' or 'Mommy' I'm out. 'Grandma,' "
he added in fairness, "gets a pass."
I laughed, which clearly must have meant
I thought he had a point.

Half of poetry is *Oh Dad, Oh Mom,*
or half of what I like—
take James Merrill's "The Broken Home"
or *Paradise Lost*. Think of Robert Hayden's
father stoking the fire before dawn.
Sylvia Plath chanting *Daddy, Daddy*
so many times that bad became good.
And what to do about Seamus Heaney
helping his mother peel potatoes—
are you telling me out it goes?
What about epitaphs for children?
You're saying you can't take the time
to read Ben Jonson's brave twelve-line
immortal burial of his son?

Sorry to complain, Billy;
I really ought to thank you. So few
poets these days are truly funny.
Besides, you've written elegies

for your bloodline, like the rest of us.
Admit it. Your poem “The Death of the Hat,”
which seems to be only about that
for stanza after stanza, is really
a lament for your dead father, whether
or not you knew it when you started.
Part of the charm is finding out.

Charm. Charm us please, don’t scream.
Maybe that’s what you’re asking of poets.
My father too wore hats with his suits
until JFK stopped doing it.
A poem in charming tribute to us,
those who remember midcentury
dads in hats, when “midcentury”
still referred to the twentieth, might
be in order sometime when we’re gone.
Today, though, I’ll attempt again

to write the poem I’ve failed to write
for six years, ever since he died.
My father. Jittery, somber, bored,
we whispered above his sleep until
midnight, when we all went back
to the hotel and bed. The call
came an hour after that, of course.
We dressed, drove over, and the nurse
gave us a little time in his room.
One by one we took our turn,
but nobody who preceded me
thought to tell me they were shocked
by how the old man looked:

eyes open wide now, terrible
enough, above his open mouth
locked in a silent scream—
proof that slipping into death
at last could not have been, for him,
anything like peace.
They shouldn't have let me see this, I thought.
They shouldn't have let me come.
I actually thought that, as if to shield
a part of me long dead, a child.
I'm writing about the shame.

NOSTALGIA

The pang for home: your roots in some other language.
Saudade, as it's said. The happy/sad of *nostos*—
the dumb tail-thumping dog; her hand-me-down
cameo ring on your own hand, evoking
a buried joy, her treble flights of laughter.
Her delight in you. You who were very young.
But you're still living, aren't you? Isn't that home?

You don't actually want to be back there, no.
There was bickering sorrow, more than you credit now.
You heard them behind the walls, his drone, her tears,
felt your own doubt and fear. What would become
of you when you left them? How could you find out?
Being young was what there was and took forever.
But if you did get old, could you start over?

But that's not it, either. Not why your worldly-wise
eyes fill at movies, why the corny score
rising in volume raises finale goose bumps
against your will when Dad pulls into the driveway.
Accommodation. As in home, and forgiveness.
With a basketball hoop above the big garage
and a hug with the uneasy teenaged son

who ducks away; he wants to dribble and shoot,
so that's how they're bonding as the credits roll.
It's not the basketballs. Not even the people.
Your pain is that again you understand
the shifting, slippery, benighted present
is what the past was and is; and that you'll find
that shimmering insight instantly forgotten.

4

A SINGLE CRYSTAL

Sylvain Tesson and Vincent Munier

It's the end of the documentary
in which two Frenchmen

(one writer, one photographer,
each of them well regarded

in the distant, overpeopled world
of galleries and book tours)

have spent uncounted subzero hours
in the mountains of Tibet

and among a few Tibetans
who sometimes come into the frame

despite the lion's share
of film time for the lonely pair

of backpacking explorers trekking
on stippled outcrops of rock,

picking their way
in snow-feathered air

across flats of ice,
squinting through wool-wrapped telescopes,

pitching camp, eating vacuum-packed
meals warmed up by karate chop,

then rigging their own video
camera to run nonstop

in their sleep through an eye-shaped
slit in the tent

in case some day-shy animal
drops by (as now and then one does,

pupils eerily hollowed out
by the night camera light),

and again breaking camp,
waking next time in a metal hut

to follow the roaming, ruglike yaks
with horns like bicycle handlebars,

or antelopes with straight horns as thin
as twinned antennae,

and while watching them,
whispering philosophically

behind a ridge
serving as their makeshift blind

that this whole extreme experience
has not been about

their own ambitions, has not been
only about their seeing other

creatures, but also about being
seen (though often unaware)

by creatures for whom
the hardly-ever-spotted human

must be bizarre as the bharal
(blue sheep-goat) is to us

and in extolling
"the art of patience"

they have just arrived
at a consensus

that it would strangely be OK
if they never happened

upon the one
living trophy they most desire

when the two men finally get
what they've come so far for,

as unlikely as Godot:
the magnificent snow leopard.

And indeed they came already knowing
this is what Peter Matthiessen

never saw in Tibet, but
found here fifty years ago,

summing up his book's
wisdom by that paradox.

Solitary, in silhouette
high on a sun-blocking cliff,

regal, tall as myth made real,
she is the object of their quest

and somewhere along the way
became mine, and yet

stubbornly I've remained
too human; I'm both enthralled

and detached enough to comprehend
I can barely stand

another minute
stranded in the grandeur of nowhere

and here's the other thing: I've been
transfixed for nearly

two hours every time the stubbled
movie-star face

of the marveling photographer
appears in superlative resolution

(every pore, every faint
crow's-foot recorded lovingly)

so that, when the beast arrives as herself
but also as removed, improved,

enlargeable in his viewfinder,
I'm seized with wonder

at how instantly the leopard moves
Munier to weep

a single crystal,
which on falling has frozen

to his right upper eyelid.
I doubt he can feel it

but I can; unable
to wipe it away

or to offer anyone anything,
I think of the lost years I was young

and life was for wasting;
liking myself

to look in mirrors,
I'd go into a shop with

almost no money
and buy, say, imitation diamonds

to glint from the holes
in my ears.

5

THE MAILMAN

Here comes the mailman. I mean the letter carrier—
the gendered term rebranded by some clever
ad person with one foot in anachronism,

since nobody writes letters. And yet our mailman
is a living, panting exemplar of hard copy,
large as a mountain climbing another mountain

as he heaves himself up our uneven stone front steps
and jams the environmentally unfriendly
unwanted catalogs into the slot.

All the time talking, loud. *That's* what I'm *sayin',*
he's saying. The earbuds nestled in his ears
listen and nod. I've always wondered who's in there,

his wife, his brother, a few good friends on call
perpetually to murmur the things you say
to someone fired up all day. When he had Covid

for two months during lockdown—almost died,
his mild replacement told us—I felt sorry
I'd never asked his name. His name is Kevin

and if he spots me through the window, always
smiles and waves, though he can't stop to talk—
to me, that is. He's otherwise engaged.

That's what I'm saying. He and I are persons,
almost outdated, not quite finished saying
whatever it is: some burning, urgent thing.

YOGA CLASS

Thank you for coming here today.
For sharing your being with us. For your commitment
to this age-old source of wisdom.
Breathe in from the depth of your diaphragm
and exhale, slowly.
Stand tall in the Mountain Pose.
Your strong feet are planted in the earth.
The top of your head is being pulled
to the top of the sky.
Think about your intentionality.

Now take one of your blocks
and come down to sit on it, like this.
Maybe you can open up your hips
so your knees touch the mat. Maybe you can't.
Whatever is right for you.
Rest your arms at your sides, feeling it,
experiencing whatever is true
for you at this time.

As you slowly, slowly begin to perform
an unnatural act I may at some point
have recommended, involving
your bent left leg and extended left arm,
you should be aware
that the rest of us are now on all fours
and our spines have all been curled into Cat Pose
before we revert to Cow. Try not to think
about taking out the trash.
Yes, you forgot it, in your rush to arrive here.
Forget that you forgot it.

Forget the ungrateful thing
the teenager in your house dared to say this morning.
Forget your foulmouthed reply.
Thank you for being wholly in this moment.

A while ago I asked you to splay your fingers
against this wall
in the Criminal Being Frisked Pose.
Yes, go ahead and imitate your neighbor.
Everything is all right. Relax.
In our practice there is no judgment.
The person in front of you is flabby
out there in the world, where people judge,
she looks unfit,
but it's clear she understands the poses
and does them with uncommon grace,
way better than you.
You back there, the poet.

You're not, I'm sensing, fully with us now,
and I'm noticing my own intention
to wipe that smirk off your face.
You're mentally at your desk already,
hunching over the screen of your laptop,
tap-tapping away,
exactly what ruined your back, which is why
you showed up here in the first place.
Could you consider resting your hands
palms up, in your actual lap?
Could you please consider never writing this poem?

STILL LIFE, HILTON HEAD

No, not a log
on the bank that rises
from the lagoon—

an alligator!
Just one shade browner
than the pristine

golf-course green
of this lawn-mown,
laundered neighborhood.

An alligator
just feet away—
undead, unfunnily

playing possum
as if an exterior
decorator

had staged it there
like a polar bear
rug or a chair;

or as if some matron
had pinned on the mound
of her bosom

a jeweled, enameled,
allegorical
alligator

she'd picked up
at a museum shop.
Don't touch! The rich

won't hurt you
if you don't
hurt them.

MRS. FLOWERS

Five minutes before the concert begins.
I'm sitting next to some old guy—
even older than I—
and ask a few idle questions.

Does he live nearby?
Oh, did he walk then?
I walk that street, I know his view—
right on a little public garden.

Nothing fancy, and yet delightful.
I picture the spring newlyweds
posing for photographers
before beds of tulip and daffodil

or under the bridal canopies
of cherry trees;
billowing picnic blankets kept
from flying away

by babies, set down like paperweights . . .
but I don't go into that; he knows it.
It's wonderful the city supports it
is all I say.

No, he explains, the funds are private.
Or they are now. Didn't used to be.
Really? It turns out he was chair
of the garden committee

for years and years
and he had it on authority
nobody else who worked on the city
budget had been aware

a little fund for the garden was in it.
Don't rock the boat,
don't ask for more, or
that pittance will be taken away:

that's what his source had said.
And then that city bureaucrat quit.
He happened to be replaced—get this—
by someone named Mrs. Flowers.

Mrs. Flowers! The old man
laughs at the thought of her, the dragon.
She cut the garden fund at once—
Cut Flowers, they called her—and ever since

the locals, or those who can, donate
money or time. A happy ending—
or not quite that; a funny one
about killjoys, who always sort of win.

The string quartet is tuning up;
it sounds like whining,
the sort of thing
people tend to do on committees

before one person has the sense
to call for silence.
The old man and I defer to it
with a seasoned nod

as people in the neighborhood
had to Mrs. Flowers.
And went on waiting for the music
and planting flowers.

CONCERTO NO. 1 FOR HEARING AIDS

walking out of the doctor's   floorboards creaking
squeaking rubber soles   then rough macadam
parking lot pebbled   evidently newly
the crunch of   crumpled   papers in her purse
until she found by feel   the key ring   lifted
jingle bells   wow   a whole percussion section
pressing the fob   the door-lock pop   ear-popping

slammed the door   shut not   meaning to said sorry
to nobody but herself   said   stuff again
to hear that person   talking loudly   tinny
hollow but tinny   and what a fussbudget   dotting
the *i*   crossing the *t*   enunciating
as if her listener were   some sort of dimwit
herself then   turned   the key in the ignition

and the radio was   on and violins
on the classical station   violins were treble
and how long had music   things   been out of whack
too   much bass too   muffled dark and sorry
treble was young   treble was   what she'd had
when she couldn't hear yet   what the world would sound
like being old   a new thought   think of that

SILENCES

Joseph Harrison, 1957–2024

Silence was not your thing.
Convivial raconteur,
your long, elaborate tales
interrupted only
by the sputtering gales
of your own helpless laughter,
ace of hosts, multitasking
griller of sizzling steaks
and topper-up of wineglasses,
commander of statistics
on politics, film, baseball,
effortless memorizer
of the Complete Plays of Shakespeare:
evenings with you were classes
in how one—no, somebody,
you—might say it all.

But oh, that final week
at home in your hospital bed—
white-sheeted and white-gowned,
the papery white skin
of your right hand peeping out,
never to write again,
asleep, your slackened mouth
emitting not a sound
but that shallow, wordless breath . . .

it seemed beyond belief
you were living but denied
your essence, which was to speak.
Then I thought: *I wasn't there.*
Not for the many hours
of silence in your life,
nobody else around,

tortured, invigorating
pauses all the times
you were working out the puzzles
of sonnets and villanelles,
unearthing puns and rhymes
that had always lain there, waiting
to be moved into the places
you newly had discovered:
even the heartbreaks
you silently endured
became mind games, high-stakes
ways to pick up the pieces
and be grateful, even happy.
I'm reading those poems, Joe,
alone and aloud; I'll see
if it helps me let you go.

6

THE FLAGELLATION

Facial expression is so unnecessary and sometimes so embarrassing that I often prefer a statue without a head.

—BERNARD BERENSON, *Piero della Francesca: The Ineloquent in Art*

The faces are famous,
partly because they seem barely variant
versions of one face—

as heavy-lidded
awake as asleep, forthright even when
gazing offstage,

unsmilingly mild
in fulfillment, unruffled by distress:
in a nutshell,

what they wish is less
to hide from expression than to express
their hiddenness.

•

Faces on a pillar
of neck always thicker than you'd expect.
Rock-solid rondure

in Mary, whether
openly pregnant or postpartum
with that hefty baby;

in Magdalene cradling
her jar of ointment, penitent;
in bearded Constantine

in his tent dreaming
between his pike-wielding sentinels;
in the dozing soldiers

not startled yet
by the torso-pierced Christ, burst from his tomb
with every limb taut and fit,

an iteration
even fitter than in life, when a younger
loinclothed ascetic

was baptized by John
in the barefoot, transparent freshness of
a swerve in the Jordan.

•

That last on the list
was my first Piero. London: back then
the revelation

was how the dove
of the Holy Ghost mirrors winglike, white
cirrus clouds that turn

into spirit, as much
as the other way round; lately I'm thinking
of the tilted cup

above the head
of Jesus, one blessed water drop
about to fall

(like the miracle
of rain out of the blue) in an undrawn
plumb line from

the bird's diving beak:
a mathematician's symmetries
dovetailed with meaning.

•

Perspective is,
Piero seems to say, impartial:
it's the vanishing

point in history
for painting figures of importance
on a grander scale

than ordinary
others who happen to share their plane.
Which is how his late

and smallish panel
The Flagellation caught me, though
merely a plate

in black and white,
reproduced, reduced, in a book by someone
also mystified

by the composition.
Urbino, I read, was where to go—
to the ducal palace

of Piero's patron
Federico da Montefeltro,
one of the few

of the artist's subjects
peggable as a portrait, the boxer's
broken nose

incongruous
as he knelt armored in prayer before
the Madonna's crowd

of saints in Milan
or faced, in Florence, the serenely neutral
profile of his

dead wife brought to life
for eternal pairing. But I digress.
What I wanted

was to find the painted
torturers shown in their true colors,
to press my nose

as close as glass
or a guard would countenance, to see
if my first impression

held: that this
Italian master anticipated
Auden's Brueghel,

who would bury the lede
about suffering largely by drowning little
Icarus in detail.

•

I went to Urbino.
For eight minutes or so, I was the sole
living person on

the planet to witness
the victim waiting in the wings
as in a corps de ballet:

feet in position
for steadiness, rounded arms with elbows
elegantly bent:

I missed at first
that his hands were bound behind that column.
Nobody came

to stop the two
flagellants, one on each side, or to stop
my looking. State-of-the-art

lighting, a bench
the proper distance away for study.
To be accurate,

nothing was happening
any more than in London, where the arm
of the soon-to-be-

beheaded Baptist
is forever raised to bless. But here
expectancy was fear,

the gruesome aim
to convince you that you almost want
the uplifted whips

to come down because
you're human. Vicious. Violent.
Impassive Pilate

presiding on his throne
to the left; meanwhile the turbaned middle-
manager type

walking not away
but toward the action, his robes in flowing
folds behind him:

they may as well
be statues for all you could ask of them.
Above the tiny head

of Jesus, a sculpted
mystery even more miniature,
like a golden

athletic trophy,
grabs my attention: a hero holding
up in triumph

his own trophy of
the globe. Apollo? Anyway,
a bystander to forgive:

he's a crafted thing
himself, he comes from before it happened.
I lean closer in,

can see the fluted
columns holding up the room
grooved in two different

tints of white,
constructing shape from shadow that
long ago began

to disintegrate:
the craquelure of paint like the threat
of an imminent

earthquake, when all
will come tumbling, crumble into dust.
But not yet: look—

•

Here's a pack of kids,
twelve-year-olds, piling up on the floor.
Their gray-haired teacher

throws out some riddles
unsolved for more than five centuries:
why are these large,

anonymous men
in the right foreground just standing around?
Why do they turn

their backs to the crime
which, surely, they can hear behind them
through the open loggia?

Or do they live in a time
long after Jesus, like us? You noticed
they're wearing clothes

of the quattrocento:
yes. But what about the angelic
one in the center

whose head is haloed
in curls and, behind them, the deep green leaves
of that laurel tree?

Why has he no shoes?
His robes are red: could that mean blood?
Bravi, ragazzi,

the young man is dead:
Federico's half brother, murdered,
some people said,

by order of
the duke himself . . . I know something about
where the story goes

from here, the ingenious,
mutually exclusive theories
involving names

even more arcane.
Regardless, that ethereal young
man not attending

even to the two
older counselors who go on droning
directly into

left ear and right
can't help but rise (as beauty does)
to become the focal point.

And does he gain
in proportion now because the face
of Jesus is,

whatever it once was,
half-stripped? The skin of paint is slashed
away across

the nose and mouth,
some art restorer's well-meant swipe
worse than the lash—

nothing to be done.
Erasure even for him. Pure ineloquence
finally has won.

•

Outside, the piazza
has filled with young men and women: today
the university

sent out into the sun
new graduates, not in mortarboards
but in the Classical

wreaths of laurel.
Every one of them looks like a god.
Stumbling, tipsy,

laughing at nothing
they'll remember, they take central places
at long tables set

for what seems a last
pizza feast with each other, planned
and paid for by

forbearing parents
and, here and there, an ambassador
from a generation

almost gone:
grandmothers wobbling in heels unwise
for cobblestones,

old men in suits
telling tales with liver-spotted hands.
I've grown sentimental,

am liable
to break into applause when I hear
the honorees

teased with their titles:
Dottore! Dottoressa! How loud
and insistent living is,

how overwrought
its twisting postures—as in an immense,
overhasty canvas

by some justly minor
mannerist—after an afternoon
spent with the still-

unlocked Piero.
The wounded grace. The self-possession.
The refusal of any

final examination
of those faces: no answer at the end.
A gust of wind

and my eye is caught
by two laureates, barely out of girlhood,
saving the day:

a pink bow has come
untied, a wreath must be set again
atop the head

of the shorter friend—
both of the tall one's arms, for a moment,
memorably suspended.

7

WE'RE DONE

Daily, with the rising of the sun,
I reach for my phone to scan the news, and it's
always the first thing I say: *We're done.*

The fires, the droughts, the icecaps warmed to run
like a bitter ice cream cone, the heedless twits
daily, with the rising of the sun,

tweeting their rights while children die and gun
sales climb, and a hobbled Congress sits
on its hands and sighs again, *We're done, we're done . . .*

It is finished, Jesus said, but then the Son
of God gets to go to Heaven. Opinion splits
with the atom, with the rising of the sun

on the Japanese flag a reimagined vision:
one bomb to end all bombs. We're in the pits
by now, dear earthly friends, *We're done, we're done.*

Intelligence deliberately spun
by humans out of range, the bytes and bits
daily, with the rising of the sun,

outthinking us? They said it at Verdun,
at Carthage, Gettysburg, and Austerlitz,
and meant it when they cried, *We're done, we're done*

but battles lost back then meant someone won.
I'm going down with poems. Though my wits
decline with every rising of the sun,
daily I still say, *We're done, we're done.*

BABY BLUE

Dozing, twitching to untellable dreams
of raising your mouth to your mother's breast
or maybe of earlier liquid long months flailing
in the womb, finally settling
head-down for a while,

you don't often show your eyes, born baby blue.
Alertness catches you several times a day
by our measure, moments we seize upon
with both hands at the back
of your funnily slumpy neck

to look into you like a pool of dark blue water.
Ink blue: that's their color on day seven,
inky irises thinking of turning brown,
much the way your ginger
head-fuzz ponders blondness.

Change is coming. But oh the stilled attention
when a grown-up thumb the very length of the sole
of your foot gently strokes it; or two thumbs,
one for each sole: your eyes
could hardly be wider

as they say to us *What is this? What, new kinds
of pleasure?*—which is, we see, precisely
what you supply by means of that blissed-out gaze,
even though you are not
at all our first baby

and once, in some unremembered time, we were you.
Newness arrives as if there's never
been anything new before: that's what we
are startled to gain again, the dozed-
off gift you wake us up for.

BLUE BABY

David Schweizer, 1950–2024

Blue baby, of the first generation
whose hole in the heart could be closed

in an operating theater
where the show must and did go on,

you thought yourself lucky as a sickly
child, who got to spend whole days

reading long books in bed.
An early obsession with Louis Seize

and the costume drama of Versailles
made you the director you were,

blocking actors in your head.
Or so we believed; you told good stories.

Long after you stopped dyeing your hair
and even your beard blood-red

and began to look your part
as a gray—no, a silver—eminence

who signed off emails "with MANLY love
from your SILVERY D,"

nevertheless you remained the *boy*
slipping out from *flamboyance,*

dressed every day in animal prints—
zebra tie, leopard sneakers, tiger

blazer, ocelot ascot. Not
just one, and often all at once.

Now it's one of your nephews who
directs us to a pew in the chapel,

now it's your beloved PAL
Caleb making his way through tears

to the pulpit, to sum up the years.
David, how can this be?

Strangely, you are not in charge.
How, on this frigid January

morning, as we stand in the snowy
churchyard where they took your body,

could there be already a hole in the heart
of the earth so large?

FIRST MEMORY

She can hold up four fingers: she understands
that next month she'll be four.
Already she remembers scenes, so many—
her mother walking in through the front door
with her wrapped-up baby brother;
that time the big dog gobbled up her toast
before she could take a single bite; that day
a bad man pushed her so hard on the swing
she spun out, landing facedown in the dust.
Also, sometimes, some first happy thing
she barely senses anymore—
a soapy bath toy, warm in her baby hands?

All of that has made her who she is
right now, a girl with pictures in her head
from a place he called the South,
her grandfather whose house she plays outside
where there's a falling whiteness that her mouth
takes in as ice cream: of all her memories
this is the first one she will claim
even into old age. How could she know
that everything that's happened until now
would melt away in time,
except the snow?

SO GLAD SHE DIDN'T LIVE TO SEE IT

What will it be, the thing they say
they're glad to have me gone before,
something I wouldn't understand
or would defeat me even more
after it was explained?

I don't mean only the generic
tragedies built into events—
fatal rare illnesses or freak
statistically sound accidents
that might take people I once loved

in life, and I'd have died again
to be told of; I mean the unique
tools and toys of daily custom—
the bound foot, or the selfie stick—
accepted by each generation

in its own time and place as not
just perfectly normal but—for all
the thought we put into it—eternal;
and go on assuming that, despite
the accelerating rate at which

we invent, adopt, get bored, discard.
So glad she didn't live to see it . . .
That's what I say in thanks my friend
Amy never had to spend
a single hour on the internet,

she who had found the typewriter
gone electric too much to bear.
I used to shrug off fears like hers
as alarmist, the inevitable
firewalls of the old and feeble—

and maybe they were. Still, the past
she lived is a thing I recognize.
Will whoever is around to mourn
my grandchildren be known at least
as human, of other humans born,

no avatar or algorithm
of buying trends or phantom-limb
expressions of feeling? Not a robot
self-taught to simulate regret?
I wonder if somehow they'll mean it,

having cannibalized the countless
metadata that incorporated
you and me, when they say of us
Poor things, they thought they were farsighted!
It's good they went when they did.

DOG WALKER

She must be ninety
if she's a day,

stepping out
this sunny morning

in golf skirt, tennis
shoes, and visor,

with a leash attached
to one handlebar

of her wheeling walker
so that her mini-

dachshund, with
like dignity,

can go his own way,
if not far.

WE SHALL ALL BE CHANGED

Locked in the vault of the cathedral
the rubies, emeralds, and sapphires
of stained glass in their upright coffers.

Locked in my throat the shards of tears.
I was one among the audience
who rose for the Hallelujah Chorus

and sang our hearts out when we came to
And He shall reign forever and ever
just before intermission, which

feels each year like the time to leave—
the heavenly overtones not over,
ringing in the ear. But now

Behold, I tell you a mystery
asserts the manly solo voice,
within the ups and downs a bass

line of authority: *the dead*
shall be raised incorruptible
and we shall all be changed.

Every time, that's when I cry
or almost cry: the threat or promise
of alteration from on high,

I who was once a first soprano
in a men's choir running short on boys,
settling for us girls because

our voices wouldn't break like glass.
Not all at once; not *in the twinkling*
of an eye; just the daily sinking

of girlishness, unperceived, into
the depth of a woman's seasoned alto,
destined not to remain the star

but to end as harmony, the friend.
No harm in that; my tears held back
are of gladness, mostly, an *amen*

for everything I've already been,
all versions vividly retained
or forgotten; and a buried prayer

that when next year's last trumpet sounds
I will not be so much changed
as not to sing my range.

Acknowledgments

Immense gratitude, as always, to my editor, Deborah Garrison. Thanks also to the editors of the journals and websites where the following poems first appeared, sometimes in slightly different form:

"Concerto No. 1 for Hearing Aids," "The Mailman," "Reflections," "Silences," and "Vaccine" in *Able Muse*
"The Flagellation" in *The American Scholar*
"First Memory" in *The Atlantic*
"Not on Speaking Terms" in *Bennington Review*
"Recovery" in blog.bestamericanpoetry.com
"Aqueduct" in *The Common*
"Full Moon" and "An Alley in Avignon" in *Commonweal*
"Christ Taking Leave of His Mother" in *The Hopkins Review*
"Baby Blue," "A Single Crystal," and "We're Done" in *Italian Americana*
"Dead Family Members," "Nostalgia," and "We Shall All Be Changed" in *Liberties*
"Two Refusals" in *Literary Matters*
"Blue Baby" in *The New Yorker*
"Still Life, Hilton Head" in *The New York Review of Books*

"So Glad She Didn't Live to See It" in *Plume*
"Mrs. Flowers" in *The Sewanee Review*
"Cameo Appearance," "Dog Walker," "Pax Romana," and "Yoga Class" in *The Southern Review*
"Home Office" in *The Wall Street Journal*

A NOTE ABOUT THE AUTHOR

Mary Jo Salter is Professor Emerita in The Writing Seminars at Johns Hopkins University. She is the author of nine previous poetry collections and a children's book, and is a co-editor of *The Norton Anthology of Poetry*. She lives in Baltimore.

A NOTE ON THE TEXT

This book was set in Scala, a typeface designed by the Dutch designer Martin Majoor (b. 1960) in 1988 and released by the FontFont foundry in 1990. While designed as a fully modern family of fonts containing both a serif and a sans serif alphabet, Scala retains many refinements normally associated with traditional fonts.

Composed by North Market Street Graphics,
Lancaster, Pennsylvania

Designed by Soonyoung Kwon